A. J. 1
LIVING IN '
IN EASY STEPS

*Understanding The Masters of Enlightenment: Eckhart Tolle,
Dalai Lama, Krishnamurti, Meister Eckhart and more!*

.WORKBOOK FOR BEGINNERS

THE SECRET OF NOW SERIES
GRAPEVINE BOOKS
Third Edition 2016

The Secret of Now Series

DISCLAIMER

All rights reserved under Title 17, U.S. Code, International and Pan-American Copyright Conventions. The duplication, sharing, uploading, transfer, and/or distribution of this electronic book by use of any digital, electronic, or printed process without the explicit permission of the publisher is unauthorized.

AUTHOR: A. J. Parr

COVER PHOTO TOLLE: Kyle Hoobin (Creative Commons) See in Wikipedia

PHOTO DALAI LAMA/TOLLE: Kris Krug (Creative Commons) See in Wikimedia Commons

PUBLISHED BY: Grapevine Books (Ediciones De La Parra)

Copyright © A. J. Parr 2014-15. All Rights Reserved.

ISBN-13: 978-1532738173

ISBN-10: 153273817X

I N D E X

FOREWORD
Page 1

LEVEL ONE: THE APPRENTICE
Page 13

LESSON 1: THE VEIL OF DELUSION
Page 15

FIRST EXERCISE: OBSERVING YOUR THOUGHTS
Page 27

LESSON 2: THE DUAL NATURE OF MAYA
Page 33

SECOND EXERCISE: COUNTING YOUR THOUGHTS
Page 39

LESSON 3: THE CHATTERING MIND
Page 47

THIRD EXERCISE: AWAKENING THE SILENT OBSERVER
Page 53

LEVEL TWO: PRACTITIONER
Page 61

LESSON 4: THE NATURE OF THE EGO AND THE SELF
Page 63

FOURTH EXERCISE: EXPERIENCING THE GAP
Page 75

LESSON 5: THE ILLUSION OF WORDS AND THOUGHTS
Page 79

FIFTH EXERCISE: EXPERIENCING YOUR INNER BODY
Page 97

LESSON 6: THE ILLUSION OF TIME
Page 101

SIXTH EXERCISE: BREATHING MEDITATION
Page 113

LEVEL THREE: THE MASTER
Page 118

LESSON 7: A TRIP BACK HOME
Page 121

SEVENTH EXERCISE: THE AWAKENING TECHNIQUE
Page 129

ABOUT THE AUTHOR
Page 141

FOREWORD

ABOUT THIS WORKBOOK

"In essence there is and always has been only one spiritual teaching, although it comes in many forms".

Eckhart Tolle

THESE PAGES CONTAIN seven basic lessons and exercises you can easily apply to help you stop your *chattering mind* and begin to experience the Now, a practice that can grant you inner peace and joy STARTING TODAY!

Here you will learn the basic principles and methods behind the ancient practice of *Living in the Now*, priceless basis of the world´s ancestral spiritual teachings, including those of Jesus, Buddha,

Krishna, Lao Tzu, Kabir, and more recently those of Eckhart Tolle, Krishnamurti, Dalai Lama, Ramana Maharshi, Maharishi Mahesh Yogi, Alan Watts, and countless others.

The seven lessons and exercises you will find are based on the following ancient premises:

> *Human suffering and unhappiness are produced by our *"chattering mind"*, which unceasingly produces an inner dialogue or chatter, preventing us from experiencing the Now.

> *There is a way to slow down and stop our chattering mind. Once you learn how to do this, you too will be able to slow down and stop it when needed (especially when you sincerely need to stop it and end your distress and self-inflicted suffering.

> *You cannot stop your thoughts completely, nor is it desirable. Even enlightened beings need to live and interact with society, like all humans.

> *By actually slowing down your chattering mind, you can make them lose their power. Simply recognize them as *"illusions"*, that is,

> products of a psychological phenomenon common among humans and allegedly known in India since prehistoric times: the phenomenon of mental illusion caused by what for thousands of years has been known as "*the veil of Maya*".

> *Only by breaking yourself free from this mental veil you can gradually awaken and free yourself from the psychological illusion that causes human suffering and unhappiness, opening the doors of your inner peace and discovering the joy of Living in the Now!

THE ANCIENT SPIRITUAL WAY OR PATH

One of the facts that most impressed me during my 30 years of Comparative Religion research is that the world's most important religions did not start out as religions but as what their ancient founders called *spiritual paths*. Surprisingly, Jesus, Buddha, Krishna, Lao-Tse, and Kabir, among other ancient founders of religions, each described his particular teachings as the "*Way*" or "*Path*" in spite of living in very different times and places, as we shall see:

> *The oldest religion in the world, presently known as Hinduism, which's ancestral pre-Vedic roots allegedly date back to the late

Stone Age, was originally known as *Sanathana Dharma* or *Perennial Way*.

Around 2,500 years ago Buddha ("Awakened One"* in Sanskrit) also centered his personal spiritual teachings on the *Dharma* or *Way,* borrowing the Sanskrit term from the Hindus, often defined as the *Way or Path to Awakening or Enlightenment.*

*At least two other ancient world religions derived from Hinduism also adopted the term *Dharma* or *Way,* including Sikhism founded by Guru Nanak (15th Century AD) and Jainism.

*The ancient Chinese based their main philosophies and religions on the concept of what they called the *Tao* (also known as *Dao*), translated as the *"Way"* or *"Path"*, basis of the Taoist teachings of Lao-Tze (6th Century BC).

*The Islamic order of the *Sufis*, the mystical or esoteric branch of Islam officially founded by the prophet Muhammad (7th Century AD) is commonly described as *"the Pathway to Allah"*.

*Similarly, according to the *Book of Genesis*, Abraham and the first Prophets of Israel practiced the *Way of the Lord* or *Way of God,* later kept hidden from the masses and which, according to esoteric tradition, served as fundamental basis of the millenary secret teachings of the Temple, from which later derived the *Kabala*, also known as the *Path of Kabbala*.

*Last but not least, the primitive disciples of Jesus and the apostles (years before receiving the name of *Christians*) were originally known, among other names, as *the sect of the Way,* as evidenced in *Acts 9,* among other scriptural testimonies:

"Meanwhile, Saul was still breathing out murderous threats against the Lord's disciples. He went to the high priest and asked him for letters to the synagogues in Damascus, so that if he found any there who belonged to the Way, whether men or women, he might take them as prisoners to Jerusalem."

The Secret of Now Series

THE ART OF LIVING: A THREE-STEP PATH

I have always liked the way the German psychoanalyst Eric Fromm describes the basic steps of learning the *Art of Living* in his best-selling book "*The Art of Loving*":

> "*The first step to take is to become aware that love is an art, just as living is an art; if we want to learn how to love we must proceed in the same way we have to proceed if we want to learn any other art, say music, painting, carpentry, or the art of medicine or engineering.*
>
> "*What are the necessary steps in learning any art? The process of learning an art can be divided conveniently into two parts: one, the mastery of the theory; the other, the mastery of the practice. If I want to learn the art of medicine, I must first know the facts about the human body, and about various diseases. When I have all this theoretical knowledge, I am by no means competent in the art of medicine.*
>
> "*I shall become a master in this art only after a great deal of practice, until eventually the results of my theoretical knowledge and*

the results of my practice are blended into one—my intuition, the essence of the mastery of any art."

For practical reasons, in accordance with the ancient spiritual paths of Hinduism and Buddhism, I have divided the *Path* described in these lessons and exercises in the following three different Levels or Stages:

*LEVEL 1: *THE APPRENTICE*

The new student first learns the basic theory, including that all our problems and sufferings are produced by our own mind, blinded by a veil of delusion that prevents us from experiencing the Now as well as reality "as is". In this initial level, together with the basic theory, the student learns the first exercises that will eventually allow him to develop his "inner eye" and become what is known as the silent Observer. The goal of this initial practice is to recognize the illusory nature of our "chattering mind" and begin to slow down its ever-flowing chain of thoughts.

*LEVEL 2: *THE PRACTITIONER*

After learning the basic theory and exercises, the student concentrates on practice, for only practice leads to mastery. *By adopting the state of the silent Observer and practicing the art of being Present in the Now (Mindfulness), the student begins to experience brief glimpses of "inner silence and stillness". With practice comes understanding and then the "illusory nature of his ego or false self" is revealed as well as the real essence of his true and transcendental inner Self. It does not depend on intellectual knowledge nor on our understanding or reasoning. It is a direct experience, free of illusion, also described as an awakening. So we mustn't try to grasp it with our minds nor try to understand it, for Inner Peace is a wordless experience that can only be attained here and now in total silence and inner stillness. As the students advances he or she develops a natural state of "renunciation" or "detachment" from the "world of illusion". Hindus call this stage in life* **Samnyasa,** *which in Sanskrit means "renunciation" or "abandonment".*

*LEVEL 3: *THE MASTER*

With due knowledge and sufficient practice always comes Mastery. Once the practitioner masters the ancient art of Being Present in the Now, the inner Self or Being gradually surges from within and can be personally felt –though never understood intellectually. When practicing the silent Art of Being Present, advanced practitioners may experience occasional "altered states of consciousness" as well as "non-dual states of consciousness". Known in Hinduism as "Savikalpa Samadhi", these altered states of consciousness are often described as states of "Beingness", that is, of "being aware of one's existence without thinking", characterized by bliss (Ananda) and joy (Sukha). This process implies regaining awareness of our inner Being and being continuously Present in the Now, enjoying an internalized state of awareness and inner peace often described as "awakened consciousness" or "enlightenment".

And now let's examine these three stages, one by one!

The Secret of Now Series

OM LEAD US

Om, Lead us from Illusion
Lead us from Darkness to Light
Lead us from the Fear of Death,
to the Knowledge of Immortality.
Om Peace, Peace, Peace!

(Brihadaranyaka Upanishad)

* * *

The Secret of Now Series

LEVEL ONE:
THE APPRENTICE

Introductory Teachings and Training

The new student first learns the basic theory, including that all our problems and sufferings are produced by our own mind, blinded by a veil of delusion that prevents us from experiencing the Now as well as reality "as is". In this initial level, together with the basic theory, the student learns the first exercises that will eventually allow him to develop his "inner eye" and become what is known as the silent Observer. The goal of this initial practice is to recognize the illusory nature of our "chattering mind" and begin to slow down its ever-flowing chain of thoughts.

The Secret of Now Series

LESSON 1

THE VEIL OF DELUSION

"Man, because he sacrifices his health in order to make money. Then he sacrifices money to recuperate his health. And then he is so anxious about the future that he does not enjoy the present; the result being that he does not live in the present or the future; he lives as if he is never going to die, and then he dies having never really lived."

Dalai Lama

THIS LESSON MARKS THE START of your Spiritual Journey to a better, healthier life, and a clear understanding that your personal problems, unhappiness and suffering are not caused by specific situations in your life but by "your illusory thoughts about them", that is, by "what you, in your own head, tell yourself about them".

Truth is, thanks to reason and logic, you have given birth to an imaginary World of Illusion that only exists in your mind. It is your subjective interpretation of the world from your personal perspective. A mental image, as we shall see that has replaced the real world in your mind, created and nurtured by your own thoughts, beliefs, values and judgements.

THE ANCIENT TEACHING OF MAYA

The ancient Hindu word *Maya* comes from the Sanskrit roots *"ma"* ("not") and *"ya"* ("that"), literally meaning *"not that"* or *"that which is not that"*, loosely meaning "Illusion".

As Eckhart explains, ancient Hindus represented this self-created illusion as *the veil of Maya,* a symbolic veil or curtain that distorts reality and makes humans chase vain dreams like madmen.

People do all sorts of things due to Maya´s veil of delusion:

*They are always chasing new desires and illusory –therefore unreachable- goals.

*They are always imagining a better future and the more they think about it, the more they feel unsatisfied with their present lives.

*Also they are always remembering and reliving s better or worse past moments and are therefore unable to experience the Now.

*They are always comparing themselves with others and complaining about their "unsatisfactory" achievements.

*They live a "false life", ruled by a "fake self-image", believing "they are someone they're not".

*They are always deceiving each other, unknowingly or not, as well as themselves.

Why do they do this?

Because of the golden veil of *Maya,* which distorts and blurs our vision, preventing us from "seeing" our true Nature and experiencing our true Self as well as profound inner peace.

THE MIND IS MAYA

One of India's greatest gurus of all times, Ramana Maharshi (1879–1950), once summed up the essence of the spiritual teachings of Hinduism in four simple words:

"The mind is Maya."

According to him, Maya can "possess" and sink us in a dream-like state, making us chase illusions in vain. It can also make us believe we are someone we are not, forget our spiritual duties, create unhappy using our own mechanical thoughts.

To understand the dream-like state created by Maya, the Hindu sage Swami Vivekananda (1863-1902) told the following tale about young Narada, one of the dearest disciples of the Hindu spiritual master Lord Krishna:

KRISHNA AND THE DREAM OF MAYA

Ramana Maharshi

I.

One day, as they walked through the woods, Krishna told his young disciple Narada about Maya and the veil of delusion.

"All you can think about all you see, Narada, is only an Illusion created by the veil of Maya" Krishna explained as they walked.

"I see what you mean, dear Master, but it's so hard to understand" said the young chela. *"How can everything we think about everything be false?*

"You will understand it the day you experience the Power of Maya, my child" said Krishna.

"My Lord, I want to understand" Narada said and then asked his master with his characteristic wide smile: *"Can you show me now the Power of Maya?"*

Krishna looked at the young chela thoughtfully and raised an eyebrow.

But he did not reply.

II.

A few days passed, and Krishna asked Narada to travel with him to the desert.

After walking for several miles under the intense sun, Krishna told him:

"I'm thirsty, Narada. Can you get me some water?"

"Yes, Master. I saw a small village nearby. I will go there at once and bring you some water" said the young disciple eagerly walking away with quick steps.

He knew exactly where to go.

III.

Narada entered the village in search of water. Almost immediately, one of the biggest houses powerfully drew his attention.

After knocking on the door, a most beautiful young girl opened it and stepped out with a smile.

It was the most beautiful woman Narada had ever seen!

As soon as he saw her, the young disciple he drew his characteristic wide smile on his face and immediately forgot that his Master was thirsty and waiting for his water.

The young disciple spent the rest of that day with girl. And that night he did not return to his Master.

The next morning, Narada went to see her again and they spent the whole day together, chatting and walking across her father's fields. But all that talking quickly ripened into love.

A few days later he asked her father for her hand and they got married shortly after.

IV.

Filled with overflowing happiness, Narada made the small village his new home. He found a job administering his father-in-

law's farm, bought a small house for him and his wife, and they were soon blessed by children.

Twelve years slowly passed by....

Narada wasn't the same man anymore.

His broad, characteristic smile was long gone. Now he was always complaining. He was buried in debts and didn't know what to do! In fact, sometimes he hated his life!

But one day his father-in-law died and Narada inherited the farm together with a small fortune.

All of the sudden, he had more money than he could spend!

Narada soon recovered his broad smile, as well as his deep love for life. As he seemed to think, he was very happy with his wife, his three children, his fields of crops, his numerous heads of cattle and his small fortune.

He had more than he ever dreamed of!

Everything seemed perfect!

But everything was about to change by a sudden twist of fate…

V.

One night, unexpectedly, there was a tragic flood.

It was past midnight when the village river waters rose without notice and overflowed its banks, flooding the place in the middle of the night.

It was a real tragedy!

Houses fell, many people and animals drowned, and half the village was swept away by the rush of the brutal stream.

Suddenly Narada found he trapped in his battered home, surrounded by furious waters, together with his dear wife and children.

Their house began to shake. It was about to fall in on them!

They needed to escape!

Standing by the open door, Narada held his dear wife with one hand, and with the other he grabbed two of his children. His third child, the smallest of the three, jumped fast on his shoulders.

Narada looked out the door and saw the rushing waters.

It seemed more than he could take.

But he had no choice.

Ready or not, he was about to meet his fate.

Narada stepped out the door holding his family close. But as soon as he took a few steps in the water, he found the current was too strong!

The waters struck wildly against them!

Narada stumbled and, all of the sudden, the child on his shoulders fell off and was swept away!

Narada shot a cry of despair!

Trying to grab and save his young son, he stretched out his hand instinctively... But by doing so he let go of his other two children, who were immediately carried away and the three sank in the mighty current!

Narada cried out in deep pain!

He embraced his dear wife with all his might. She was all he had left!

But the current was too strong and suddenly his wife was also torn away from him and was carried away by the mighty waters in which she sank!

He too was swept by the mighty current. He thought it was the end. Only then he remembered his dear Master Krishna. But it was too late.

VI.

Almost unconscious, Narada sank and twirled beneath the torrential waters, only to be surprisingly hurled with great force onto the riverbank!

Narada was alive!

But his pain was too strong. Weeping and wailing in bitter lamentation, he wished he was dead!

Suddenly, from behind him, there came a gentle voice: "My child, Narada. Where is my water?"

Narada turned around and was amazed to see Krishna smiling at him.

"Where is my water?" his Master repeated. "You went for water half an hour ago! And I'm still waiting!

Narada looked around him dumbfounded.

The fierce waters, the torn buildings, the few trees that were still left standing, and even the river and its bank... Everything had vanished!

"Did you say half an hour ago, Master?" Narada asked Krishna, scratching his head.

Everything seemed so unreal!

"Of course, Narada! You were only gone for half an hour!"

Narada couldn't believe it!

Twelve whole years had passed by, but only in his mind! And only in half an hour!

All he lived in those twelve years, all those days and experiences, all those joys and sorrows, all those weeks, months and years.... Everything had only been an Illusion!

"Yes, my child. It's just what you asked for, isn't it?" Krishna gently asked, placing a paternal hand on Nerada's shoulder. "Now you know the Power of Maya!"

FIRST EXERCISE

OBSERVING YOUR THOUGHTS

"Try a little experiment. Close your eyes and say to yourself: 'I wonder what my next thought is going to be.' Then become very alert and wait for the next thought. Be like a cat watching a mouse hole. What thought is going to come out of the mouse hole? Try it now."

Eckhart Tolle

THE FOLLOWING EXERCISE WILL SHOW YOU how to "Observe your thoughts", a basic step in understanding the basics of "conscious thinking" and how the veil of delusion affects us.

Remember what Eckhart recommends:

"To free yourself from Illusion and experience spiritual growth, you must become the Observer."

You can practice this exercise by yourself, as well as the rest of the exercises contained in this book. However, it´s better if you have someone else with you the first time you practice. This way he or she can read out the instructions as you exercise. Great practice for couples!

OBSERVING YOUR OWN THOUGHTS

This exercise will prepare you for the rest of the exercises contained in this workbook, specially designed to boost your spiritual growth.

To get started just follow these steps:

1:

This exercise will last less than a minute. Sit or lie down in a comfortable and relaxing position. The position you now have while reading this book will do. You can also adopt another or a meditation or yoga pose.

2:

Close your eyes. Although you can also do this exercise with your eyes open, I recommend doing it with your eyes closed this first time to avoid unwanted distractions and increase your inner concentration.

3:

No matter what you are thinking when you close your eyes, this will be your thought number one. Remember this.

For example, you may be thinking "I wonder what this exercise is all about" or "I´m hungry" or "Hey! I forgot to call mom!" What you´re thinking really doesn´t matter. Above all, here´s what you need to do:

*Realize that you are having a thought.

*Recognize your thought, that is, understand what the thought is all about. For example: "I need to go to the bank tomorrow".

4:

Once you "get the idea" or "understand your though" say "YES!" out loud.

Apart from forcing you to keep focused on the exercise, saying it out loud will also help you interrupt your thinking process briefly, which is the main purpose of the following step.

5:

If the information is important for you, like for example having to go to the bank tomorrow, take mental note of it and leave it for later. If it is not important, ignore it. In either case, to stop thinking about it jump to the next step.

6:

Immediately say to yourself, following Eckhart's instructions:

"I wonder what my next thought is going to be."

Be alert. Watch your mind. Wait for your next thought.

Like Eckhart says, "be like a cat watching a mouse hole."

7.

Very soon you will think about something or a new thought will spontaneously pop in your head. Either way, it fine.

Identify your new thought. For example: "I'm thirsty" or "What was the name of that person I met yesterday?" For the sake of this experiment, this will be your "thought number two".

8:

Don't engage in your thought. Simply be alert and recognize it. As soon as you know what your "thought number two" is about, say "YES!" out loud. This will help you interrupt your "chain of thoughts" and continue with the next step.

9:

After saying "yes", stop thinking about it. Leave it for later and let it go. Try putting your mind in "blank" and continue to the next step.

10:

Once again, follow Eckhart's instructions and mentally say to yourself:

"I wonder what my next thought is going to be."

You really don't need to say this verbally, only if you want to. Simply be alert and wait for your next thought. *"Be like a cat watching a mouse hole."*

11.

Soon a third thought will arise. It doesn't matter if your new thought is "Where did I leave my keys?" or "I'm sleepy" or "I'm having thoughts". Simply be alert and silently recognize your new thought as soon as it appears.

The co-founder of the Chopra Center, Dr. David Simon, an expert in transcendental meditation, often told his students:

"The thought *I'm having thoughts* may be the most important thought you have ever thought, because before you had that thought, you may not have even known you were having thoughts. You probably thought you *were* your thoughts."

12.

As soon as you recognize your third thought and identify what it's about, say "YES" one last time before taking a deep breath and opening your eyes.

13:

Repeat this exercise two or three times a day. Observing only three thoughts each time will do. It will take you less than half a minute. Just remember: after recognizing each new thought and saying "YES!", immediately leave it for later and stop thinking about it.

Apart from allowing you to "observe your thoughts" this exercise also teaches you how to let your thoughts go. And I cannot express how important this is when trying to slow down and stop your "unceasing mental chatter".

As you will experience in the following exercises, learning to "release" your thoughts will help you avoid engaging in an endless monologue or a mental discussion with no end and give yourself a break. And don't forget the primary purpose of these first set of exercises: **"Be present. Be there as the Observer of the mind."**

LESSON 2

THE DUAL NATURE OF MAYA

"There exists only the present instant... a Now which always and without end is itself new. There is no yesterday nor any tomorrow, but only Now, as it was a thousand years ago and as it will be a thousand years hence..."

Meister Eckhart

MAYA IS THE ANCIENT SANSKRIT WORD for thousands of years used to describe *"the state of mind in which we are prevented to experience our true Self or Ultimate Reality"*, or *"the primary phenomenon that prevents us from attaining enlightenment and realizing the true nature of all things"*. It is also the name of the Hindu goddess *Maya* or *MahaMaya, the ancient Mother of Illusion*, dreams, deceptions, and spells, which she manifests, perpetuates and governs at will. According to olden Hindu tradition, this goddess has two opposite natures: a lower or negative one and a higher or positive. Let's take a quick look at both of them:

THE LOWER NATURE OF MAYA

According to Hindu tradition, the goddess Maya is capable of tempting and captivating even the strongest man. And once she has him under her control, she reveals "her true evil form". Truth is, most people are permanently experiencing the lower essence of *Maya,* that is, her dreaded "veil of delusion".

Known as "the deceiver" or the "secret enemy", this lower essence of *Maya* can actually trap you in an imaginary dream-like state, just like the one Krishna's disciple, young Narada had when he experienced twelve years in only half an hour, as told in the first lesson.

This dream-like state, comparable to madness, is produced by our imaginary beliefs, values, joys and sorrows. Fact is, just like Narada, most of us live "imaginary lives" and, without realizing it, we vainly chase empty dreams and illusory goals; always imagining a better future or remembering a better past; and always complaining about the Now.

Also like Narada, most people end up believing we are "someone we are not", assuming false identities. We say "I am this" or "I am that". But in reality, due to the veil of Maya, most of us don´t even know who or what we truly are!

THE HIGHER NATURE OF MAYA

According to Hindu teachings, the higher nature of *Maya* has a "positive" and "transcendental" purpose, for it serves us as "spiritual teacher" and "giver of superior knowledge".

As experience shows, "deception often leads to truth". This is why in Hindu tradition the goddess Maya is also known as the "giver of awareness" and "bringer of evolution". Its higher essence, instead of sinking you deeper in the world of illusion, can actually help you "wake up from the dream" and reach the road to enlightenment.

How?

Find out in the following pages!

AND THIS IS MĀYĀ

Swami Vivekananda

Hope is dominant in the heart of childhood. The whole world is a golden vision to the opening eyes of the child; he thinks his will is supreme. As he moves onward, at every step nature stands as an adamantine wall, barring his future progress. He may hurl himself against it again and again, striving to break through. But the further he goes, the further recedes the ideal, till death comes, and there is release, perhaps. **And this is Māyā.**

The senses drag the human soul out. Man is seeking for pleasure and for happiness where it can never be found. For countless ages we are all taught that this is futile and vain, there is no happiness here. But we cannot learn; it is impossible for us to do so, except through our own experiences. We try them, and a blow comes. Do we learn then? Not even then. Like moths hurling themselves against the flame, we are hurling ourselves again and again into sense-pleasures, hoping to find satisfaction there. We return again and again with freshened energy; thus we go on, till crippled and cheated we die. **And this is Māyā.**

So with our intellect. In our desire to solve the mysteries of the universe, we cannot stop our questioning, we feel we must know and cannot believe that no knowledge is to be gained. A few steps, and there arises the wall of beginningless and endless time which we cannot surmount. A few steps, and there appears a wall of boundless space which cannot be surmounted, and the whole is irrevocably bound in by the walls of cause and effect. We cannot go beyond them. Yet we struggle, and still have to struggle. **And this is Māyā.**

With every breath, with every pulsation of the heart with every one of our movements, we think we are free, and the very same moment we are shown that we are not. Bound slaves, nature's bond-slaves, in body, in mind, in all our thoughts, in all our feelings. **And this is Māyā.**

(Delivered in London, 22nd October 1896)

* * *

The Secret of Now Series

SECOND EXERCISE

COUNTING YOUR THOUGHTS

"You have probably come across 'mad' people in the street incessantly talking or muttering to themselves. Well, that's not much different from what you and all other "normal" people do, except that you don't do it out loud."

Eckhart Tolle

ACCORDING TO ECKHART TOLLE, we cannot experience the Power of Now unless we learn to stop our unceasing "mental dialogue or chatter":

*A chatter that is always about the past or about the future, but hardly about the present.

*A chatter that always distracts you and always triggers more thoughts.

*A chatter that prevents you from experiencing the "Now"!

Unfortunately, most people are unaware of this. But how on earth can they be aware of it if they're always too busy, endlessly speaking in their minds?

COUNTING YOUR THOUGHTS:

Minute by minute, hour by hour, and day by day, your "mental chatter" sinks you deeper in the illusory world of Maya. The following exercise will allow you to calculate how many involuntary thoughts you have in a minute or so.

You will need the following:

*A calculator.

*A stopwatch or something to keep track of time.

Someone to assist you, basically so he or she can keep track of the time while you concentrate on the exercise. You can also take turns if you want.

PART ONE OF THE EXERCISE

1:

Sit or lie down in a comfortable and relaxing position. The position you now have while reading this book will do or a meditation or yoga pose if you like.

2:

Close your eyes. You can do this exercise with your eyes open, but with eyes closed you will avoid distractions and increase concentration.

3:

No matter what you're thinking about when you close your eyes, that will be your "thought number one", just like in our last exercise.

For example you may be thinking "I wonder what this exercise is all about" or "I'm hungry" or "Wow! I forgot to call mom!" That will be your thought number one. What you're thinking really doesn't matter. Above all, don't get involved with your thought, that is, do not turn a single thought into a "conversation" or "monologue". Simply do the following:

*Realize that you are having a thought now, in the present moment.

*Be aware of the moment. Recognize your thought, that is, understand what the thought is all about. For example: "I need to go to the bank tomorrow".

4:

Once you recognize your though, say out loud or yell the word "ONE!" (The number of the thought).

5:

Don´t engage in your thought. Recognize it, take mental note if needed, leave it for later, let it go and jump to the next step.

6:

Be alert and wait for your next thought. "Be like a cat watching a mouse hole," as Eckhart recommends. Very soon a new thought will pop in your head. This will be your "thought number two". As soon as it appears, recognize it and say "TWO!" (The number of the second thought). Immediately after saying this, stop thinking about it, leave it for later, and let it go.

7:

Continue repeating the process for exactly 60 seconds (a complete minute). No less not more.

REMEMBER:

*Each time a new idea appears, repeat the process: recognize it, say its number and let it go.

*Don't get engaged in your thoughts during the exercise.

*Keep track of the number of thoughts you have by saying each number out loud.

*When the 60 seconds are up, write down the total number.

For example: 25 thoughts (my result the first time I did this exercise).

PART TWO OF THE EXERCISE

Take out your calculator, a notebook or blank paper and a pencil or pen (You can also use your computer or laptop instead).

YOUR PER-MINUTE RATE:

Write down the number of thoughts you had in 60 seconds (one minute).

This number is what we´re really after in the first part of this exercise. It will tell you, approximately, your personal THOUGHTS PER MINUTE or TPM RATE. For example, my TPM rate the first time I did this exercise was 25 thoughts per minute.

What's your TPM rate?

*YOUR PER- HOUR RATE:

Suppose you had 25 thoughts, like I did. Take that number and multiply it by 60. This will let you know your approximate THOUGHTS PER HOUR OR TPH RATE. In my case its 25 x 60.

That's 1,500 thoughts per hour!

What's your TPH rate?

*YOUR PER-DAY RATE:

To calculate how many thoughts you have in a single day, multiply your TPH times 24. That WILL BE YOUR THOUGHTS PER DAY or TPD RATE.

For example, in my case, 1,500 times 24.

This gave me a total of 36,000 thoughts per day!

What's your TPD rate?

*YOUR PER-YEAR RATE:

Finally, multiply your TPD RATE by 365 and that will give you your approximate THOUGHTS PER YEAR or TPY RATE. In my case, 36,000 times 365.

THAT'S OVER 13 MILLION THOUGHTS IN A YEAR!

*13,140,000 thoughts per year to be exact.

*There are 525,600 minutes in a year.

*How many of these thoughts made me feel good? How many made me feel bad? How many were useful? How many were a waste of time? How many gave me inner peace and how many stressed me out? How many helped me in my Spiritual Journey and how many sank me even deeper in the world of Illusion?

And you? What´s your TPY rate?

Like I mentioned, doing this exercise allows you to measure the approximate rate of your "unceasing inner chat", which minute by minute, hour by hour, and day by day, sinks you deeper and deeper in the illusory world of Maya ...*unless you decide to do something about it!*

The Secret of Now Series

LESSON 3

THE CHATTERING MIND

"I am just asking you why does the mind chatter? Is it a habit or does the mind need to be occupied with something? And when it is not occupied with what it thinks it should be occupied, we call it chattering. Why should not the occupation be chattering also? I am occupied with my house. You are occupied with your God, with your work, with your business, with your wife, with your sex, with your children, with your property. The mind needs to be occupied with something and therefore when it is not occupied, it may feel a sense of emptiness and therefore chatters."

Krishnamurti

ACCORDING TO AN ANCIENT SAYING, if you cannot control your own mind, then your mind is actually controlling you! And that's a problem you can't afford!

The reason for not being able to control our minds is that most people are unconsciously identified with their "inner voice" and are unknowingly "slaves" of their own automatic or programmed thoughts, beliefs, values, and desires.

The Indian philosopher Jiddu Krisnamurti (1895-1986) usually referred to the thinking mind as the *"chattering mind"*, stating that this chatter is a constant process, an endless operation, and that *"every moment it is murmuring"*.

In his 1954 best-seller *"The First and Last Freedom"* he stated:

> *"As I watch the brain, I see that the chattering happens only in the brain, it is a brain activity; a current flows up and down, but it is chaotic, meaningless and purposeless. The brain wears itself out by its own activity. One can see that it is tiring to the brain, but it does not stop... The mind chatters all the time and the energy devoted to that purpose fills a major part of our life.*
>
> *"The mind apparently needs to be occupied with something... The mind is occupied with something and if it is not occupied, it feels*

vacant, it feels empty and therefore it resorts to chattering..."

Regarding the need to quiet our chattering mind and acquire the silent state of inner stillness, Krishnamurti stated:

"The still mind is the most active mind but if you will experiment with it, go into it deeply, you will see that in stillness there is no projection of thought. Thought, at all levels, is obviously the reaction of memory and thought can never be in a state of creation. It may express creativeness but thought in itself can never be creative. When there is silence, that tranquillity of mind which is not a result, then we shall see that in that quietness there is extraordinary activity, an extraordinary action which a mind agitated by thought can never know...

"The still mind is the most active mind but if you will experiment with it, go into it deeply, you will see that in stillness there is no projection of thought. Thought, at all levels, is obviously the reaction of memory and thought can never be in a state of creation. It may express creativeness but thought in itself can never be creative. When there is silence, that tranquillity of mind which is

not a result, then we shall see that in that quietness there is extraordinary activity, an extraordinary action which a mind agitated by thought can never know.

Only by observing yourself in complete stillness you will be able to actually "see" who you really are. This is why all the ancient wise men of Athens highlighted the importance of the olden maxim inscribed in the Temple of Apollo in the city of Delphi: *"Know thyself"*.

That's basically it: You must know yourself! And the best way to do this, as you will see in the following lessons, is through Self-observation, that is, by recognizing your own thoughts and learning how to slow them down and experience "inner stillness".

Remember; No one else can do this for you. Only you can!

In conclusion, to attain spiritual progress you simply need to practice and follow your heart. Simply experience things for yourself. And please don't pay attention to other people's opinions, beliefs, values and desires.

In this early stage of your spiritual training you first need to concentrate on observing the voice in your head until you are finally fit to grab the reins of your life and experience inner peace and happiness for yourself!

* * *

THE SILENT LANGUAGE

RAMANA MAHARSHI

Silence is ever-speaking,

It is the perennial flow of "language."

It is interrupted by speaking,

For words destroy this mute language.

Silence is unceasing eloquence.

It is the best language.

There is a state when words cease

And silence prevails.

* * *

The Secret of Now Series

THIRD EXERCISE

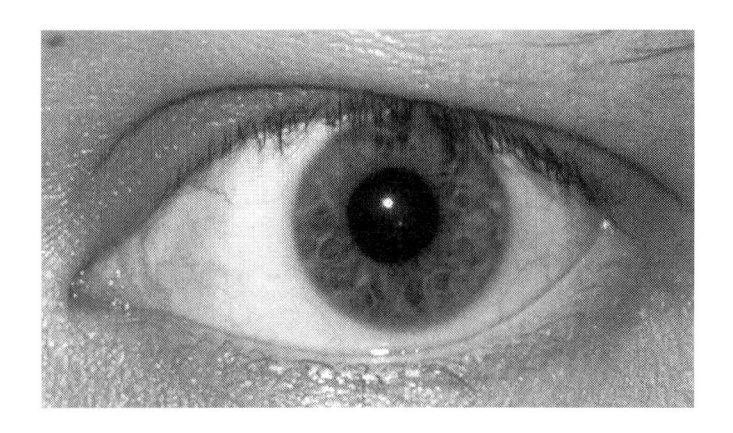

AWAKENING THE SILENT OBSERVER

"Start listening to the voice in your head as often as you can. Pay particular attention to any repetitive thought patterns, those old gramophone records that have been playing in your head perhaps for many years. This is what I mean by "watching the thinker," which is another way of saying: listen to the voice in your head, be there as the witnessing presence.

"When you listen to that voice, listen to it impartially. That is to say, do not judge. Do not judge or condemn what you hear, for doing so would mean that the same voice has come in again through the back door. You'll soon realize: there is the voice, and here I am listening to it, watching it. This I am realization, this sense of your own presence, is not a thought. It arises from beyond the mind..."

Eckhart Tolle

THE DEVELOPMENT OF YOUR INNER VISION or insight is fundamental if you seek to free yourself from the heavy load of your daily problems. As these pages evidence, most of your personal problems are *"self-inflicted"*, that is, they are illusory creations of your own mind.

In his book *"Transcendent Wisdom"*, the Dalai Lama explains that one of the basic aspects of Tibetan philosophy derives from the ancient teachings of the celebrated 8th-century monk known as Shantideva, who stated that human beings experience two basic and distinctive realities:

ILLUSORY REALITY: The first and most commonly perceived is called *"conventional reality"* or *"illusory reality"* and is basically a production or projection of our own mind or intellect. It can be described as a personal and relative view of the world based on duality and our own speculations and ideas of what this reality should be. In sum, it is only the product of our own imagination!

Illusory reality only exists within our own minds. It is like a dream or the trick of a magician, as the Dalai Lama warns in *"Transcendent Wisdom"*:

> *"While dreaming, all kinds of things may come to mind, but these are nothing more than appearances. Likewise, a magician may*

create a variety of illusory appearances, but they do not exist objectively..."

REAL REALITY: The second is subjacent and known as *"ultimate reality"* or *"real reality"*. It is everything that truly exists. It cannot be perceived by the intellect nor described in words, and can only be directly experienced by seekers of the Path who have effectively *"tamed"* their minds and developed their *"inner sight"* or *"third eye"*.

FREEING YOURSELF FROM ILLUSION

Unless we learn to recognize the falseness of our own illusory world, it will continue deceiving and sinking us in a world of suffering and hostility.

As the Dalai Lama preaches, to free ourselves from the chains of illusion, we must first learn to perceive reality as the only Truth, often referred to in ancient Buddhist scriptures as *"emptiness"* due to the fact that it cannot be described with words other than "void of form, name, shape, characteristics and beyond time and space".

Also according to the Dalai Lama, unless we experience this true reality within us, within our hearts, and stop believing in the world of verbal thinking and all the mental representations we have erected within our heads, we will inexorably continue to be blinded by the veil of illusion woven by our own ignorance. An illusion that always brings new joys and satisfactions that are always followed by new sufferings and dissatisfactions, endlessly turning like a spinning wheel that intimately affects the outcome of our daily living and very often disturbs our general wellbeing.

Recognizing and experiencing *"real reality"*, as the Dalai Lama states, is the only way of freeing ourselves from the heavy chains of illusion that cause our suffering. And once we do this, we will recognize our *"illusory reality"* as a foul dream that is not real and only then it will cease to affect our natural state of perpetual happiness and wellbeing.

OPENING THE INNER EYE

Truth is, for thousands of years the *"inner eye"*, also known as the *"eye of the soul"*, has been widely studied in India, including the followers of both Hinduism and Buddhism. But it is also said that Jesus openly referred to it in Matthew 6:22-23:

> *"The light of the body is the eye, therefore when you eye is good, your whole body is full of light; but when your eye is bad, your body is full of darkness. Take heed therefore that the light which is in you be not darkness. If thy whole body therefore be full of light, having no part dark, the whole shall be full of light, as when the bright shining of a candle does give you light."*

According to the ancient teachings of Hinduism and Buddhism, the third eye is located in the middle of the forehead and is the gate to *"the inner realms and higher states of consciousness"*. Hindu tradition associates the third eye with the *ajna*, or the chakra of the brow.

AWAKENING THE OBSERVER

Awakening the Observer or Silent Witness is a vital step when learning to tame the mind and is the object of the present exercise. It will allow you to recognize "the voice in your head" as something different from your true Self.

To begin to awaken your inner eye and adopt the state of the just follow these steps:

1:

Sit or lie down in a comfortable and relaxing position. The position you now have while reading this book will do or a meditation or yoga pose if you like.

2:

Close your eyes. No matter what you're thinking, realize that you are having a thought and identify it. Once you recognize it, say "yes" out loud and, without engaging in your thought, leave it for later and let it go as you learned to do in the last exercises.

3:

Try to keep complete mental silence for a second or two. Simple be alert and wait for your next thought. "Be like a cat watching a mouse hole," as Eckhart explains. Keep mentally silent and wait for "the voice in your head" to say something new, something spontaneous, that is, on its own and without you voluntarily participating.

4:

Very soon, despite your silence, you will hear the "voice in your head" say something new, as if it had "a will of its own". Immediately try to identify the two distinctive players that are participating within your head:

*The voice in your head.

*And you as the silent observer.

To help you identify the two players, Eckhart recommends asking yourself: "Am I the thoughts that are going through my head? Or, am I the one who is aware that these thoughts are going through my head?"

5:

Recognize the new thought before saying "yes" out loud and, without engaging in your thought, leave it for later and let it go. Repeat the process several times until you begin to experience the separation between the "voice in your head" (which uses verbal language) and you as the Observer (immersed in silence).

Remember, let "the voice in your head" do the talking. Don´t try to control it. Simply observe your mind in silence. As soon as a new idea appears, recognize it, say "yes" and let it go.

Remember:

Try to experience being the Observer, don't get engaged in your thoughts during the exercise, and prepare yourself to begin the second level of our Spiritual Journey!

The Secret of Now Series

LEVEL TWO:
THE PRACTITIONER

The Practice of Observing Presence

After learning the basic theory and exercises, the student concentrates on practice, for only practice leads to mastery. *By adopting the state of the silent Observer and practicing the art of being Present in the Now (Mindfulness), the student begins to experience brief glimpses of "inner silence and stillness". With practice comes understanding and then the "illusory nature of his ego or false self" is revealed as well as the real essence of his true and transcendental inner Self. It does not depend on intellectual knowledge nor on our understanding or reasoning. It is a direct experience, free of illusion, also described as an awakening. So we mustn't try to grasp it with our minds nor try to understand it, for Inner Peace is a wordless experience that can only be attained here and now in total silence and inner stillness. As the students advances he or she develops a natural state of "renunciation" or "detachment" from the "world of illusion". Hindus call this stage in life* **Samnyasa,** *which in Sanskrit means "renunciation" or "abandonment".*

LESSON 4

THE NATURE OF THE EGO AND THE SELF

""I'm trying to free your mind, Neo. But I can only show you the door. You're the one that has to walk through it... There is a difference between knowing the path and walking the path."

Morpheus – The Matrix

IN THE CELEBRATED FILM *MATRIX* (1999), Thomas A. Anderson is a skillful computer expert living two lives: By day he is a common computer programmer. But by night he is a secret hacker known as Neo.

Neo is a rebel. He has always questioned his present. He is unsatisfied with his reality. He definitely needs a change. But he never imagined that soon he would find out that everything he had lived in his life was only a dream!

A vain illusion just like Nerada's!

This is how Neo´s amazing and futuristic story begins:

> *Neo is contacted by Morpheus, a legendary computer hacker and known terrorist. Neo has heard a lot about him. He has always secretly admired him as his superior in age, experience, and wisdom. But he knows Morpheus only means trouble!*
>
> *Morpheus surprises Neo by suddenly asking him:*
>
> *"Have you ever had a dream, Neo, that you were so sure was real? What if you were unable to wake from that dream? How would*

you know the difference between the dream-world and the real world?"

Morpheus then tells Neo the world as they know it is only an illusory dream that veils another world.

But Neo refuses to believe it!

To convince him, Morpheus tells him what he calls "the truth":

The "illusion of this world" is a perpetual dream artificially created by an enslaving machine called The Matrix, which feeds on human bio-electricity.

"The Matrix is a computer-generated dream-world built to keep us under control in order to change a human being into this," Morpheus said, holding up a Duracell battery.

"No!" Neo exclaimed shaking his head in denial. "I don't believe it! It's not possible!

"The Matrix is everywhere" Morpheus continued saying. "It is all around us. Even

now, in this very room. You can see it when you look out your window or when you turn on your television. You can feel it when you go to work... when you go to church... when you pay your taxes. It is the world that has been pulled over your eyes to blind you from the truth."

"What truth?" asks Neo.

"That you are a slave, Neo. Like everyone else you were born into bondage. Into a prison that you cannot taste or see or touch. A prison for your mind."

* * *

Did you notice any similarities between Matrix and the world of Maya? For the purpose of this lesson, I will only point out a couple:

*The false Neo (trapped in the Illusion of the Matrix) can be compared with our "illusory self" or ego.

*The real Neo (free from the Illusion of the Matrix) can be compared with our natural Self.

Having said that, I believe the moral of the symbolic story is quite clear:

> *Only through Self-knowledge we can escape from the world of Illusion and transcend from ego to Self.*

SELF-KNOWLEDGE: THE KEY TO FREEDOM

According to the ancient teachings of Hinduism, to free ourselves from the chains the illusions of this world and attain salvation, first we must acquire Self-knowledge *(atma jnana)*.

But what did they mean by Self-knowledge?

Basically the knowledge that our true Self or Atman is not tour illusory self or ego. And that our true Self is identical with the transcendental Self we call God or Brahman: the Ultimate Reality.

The ancient rishis of Hinduism divided the study of Self-knowledge in two separate branches. But both are really One:

The knowledge of the lower animal self or ego (the psychological "I", the thinker)

The knowledge of the true Self or soul, (the transcendental "I", the Observer)

Since the dawn of mankind, these teaching have been passed down, from Master to disciple, and from generation to generation, and finally they have reached our days.

THE KNOWLEDGE OF THE EGO

According to Eckhart Tolle, *"as you grow up, you form a mental image of which you are, based on your personal and cultural conditioning. We may call this phantom self the ego."*

Eckhart's teachings, as well as the Hindu's, claim that your *"ego"* or *"rational mind"* needs constant thinking to exist. People become addicted to thinking because they are identified with their erroneous *"sense of self"*.

Building your ego is like building a castle in your imagination.

The more you think about it, the more details you will imagine and the stronger your mental image of the castle will be. Only that in this case you are the castle.

Don't take it wrong, but you are not who you think you are.

No matter what you think, the *"mental image of who you are"* is only a supposition, a speculation, an imaginary you that you have created and that you nurture with your thoughts.

But it is only an illusion!

Like I said, you're not who you think you are! The person who you think you are is only a creation of your limited mind, an image you have built since your childhood and in which you have thought all your life!

The more you think about it, the stronger it gets.

The less you think about it, the weaker it gets.

And if you stop thinking about it will reach a dormant state and disappear!

When one of his disciples asked the famous nineteenth-century Hindu mystic Ramakrishna what is the ego the wise man replied:

> *"Ponder deeply, and you will know that there is no such thing as 'I'. As you peel off the skin of an onion, you find it consists only of skin; you cannot find any kernel in it. So too on analyzing the ego, you will find that there is no real entity that you can call 'I'. Such an analysis of the ego convinces one that the ultimate substance is God alone. When egotism drops away, Divinity manifests Itself."*

THE KNOWLEDGE OF THE SELF

Atman in Sanskrit means "*Inner-Self*" or "*soul*".

The Atman is our true Self, beyond identification with phenomena. It is the higher Self, identified with the Absolute Substance or Brahman, the transcendental One, beyond space and time, formless and unchangeable.

Since the ultimate reality is that all is One, then we are all part of the One too, as well as everything that surrounds us (including the whole universe).

The only way for the Absolute to experience "individuality" is by the illusion of the ego that is by the power of Maya. Without Maya we would not be able to experience separation from the Absolute and would only experience the One. Such is the power of Maya.

But this apparent *"individuality"* or *"separation from the One"* it is only a game or Leela played by the Absolute, our true Self.

According to Hinduism:

> *The One, or Absolute: Reality, is always real.*

> *It has no form. It has no name.*

> *It is limitless. It is not bound. It is beyond space and time.*

> *It is the formless being which sustains the universe.*

It transcends speech and therefore cannot be described.

It is your inner-Self, a subjective awareness of "I am".

It is your real form (nija-swarupa).

It dwells in the center of your heart.

The Secret of Now Series

CONFUSED BY THOUGHTS

HUI NENG

Confused by thoughts,

we experience duality in life.

Unencumbered by ideas,

the enlightened see the one Reality.

* * *

The Secret of Now Series

FOURTH EXERCISE

EXPERIENCING THE GAP

"The mind is quiet when it sees the truth that understanding comes only when it is quiet; that if I would understand you, I must be quiet, I cannot have reactions against you, I must not be prejudiced, I must put away all my conclusions, my experiences and meet you face to face. Only then, when the mind is free from my conditioning, do I understand. When I see the truth of that, then the mind is quiet - and then there is no question of how to make the mind quiet."

Krishnamurti

ALTHOUGH YOUR CHATTERING MIND unceasingly speaks, generating thousands of thoughts per day, try to detect the brief space between one thought and the next: the silent gap. During these gaps, according to Eckhart, the awareness of something simply becomes the awareness of the Now.

To start experiencing these gaps, just follow the steps:

1:

Sit or lie down in a comfortable and relaxing position. The position you now have while reading this book will do or a meditation or yoga pose if you like.

2:

Close your eyes. No matter what you´re thinking, realize that you are having a thought and identify it. Once you recognize it, say "YES!" out loud and, without engaging in your first thought, leave it for later and let it go as you learned to do in the last exercises.

3:

Try to keep complete mental silence for a second or two. "Be like a cat watching a mouse hole". Before your new thought arrives, you will experience a brief blank space or gap between your first and second thoughts. It may only last a brief instant.

"Pay attention to the gap" Eckhart Tolle says in his book *Stillness Speaks*, "the gap between two thoughts, the brief, silent space between words in a conversation, between the notes of a piano or flute, or the gap between the in-breath and the out-breath. When you pay attention to those gaps, awareness of 'something' becomes just awareness. The formless dimension of pure consciousness arises from within you and replaces identification with form."

This blank or silent gap, as Deepak Chopra points out, is the home of inner peace and enlightenment. You have a thought here, a thought here, and between every thought there's a little space.

Each time a new thought arises, as it inevitably does, don't think anything else about it, don't judge it and don't try to push it away. Instead of doing this, simply "release it" and "let it go". And if you pay attention you will experience brief moments between thoughts in this space of pure awareness and silence. Initially the experience may only last a second or even brief microseconds, so pay attention.

As Eckhart Tolle explains in *A New Earth*, "you don't need to be concerned with the duration of those gaps. A few seconds is good enough. Gradually, they will lengthen themselves, without any effort on your part. More importantly than their length is to bring them in frequently so that your daily activities and your stream of thinking become interspersed with space."

In *"The Power of Now"*, Eckhart explains that *"when a thought subsides, you experience a discontinuity in the mental stream – a gap of "no-mind."* At first, the gaps will be short, a few seconds perhaps, but gradually they will become longer. When these gaps occur, you feel a certain stillness and peace inside you. This is the beginning of your natural state of felt oneness with Being, which is usually obscured by the mind. With practice, the sense of stillness and peace will deepen. In fact, there is no end to its depth. You will also feel a subtle emanation of joy arising from deep within: the joy of Being."

4:

Repeat the process several times. Concentrate on experiencing longer gaps. Don't judge your thoughts or engage in them. Just observe them, say "yes" and release them while concentrating on experiencing the gaps.

LESSON 5

THE ILLUSION OF WORDS AND THOUGHTS

"My teaching is like a finger pointing to the moon. Do not mistake the finger for the moon."

Gautama Buddha

HUMAN THINKING, AS WE KNOW, is mostly based on *"words"*, which constitute the basis or oral speech and verbal thinking.

Words, however, are only symbols. But most people seem to forget this!

The word *"moon"* for example, is used to represent the real moon. But it is not the actual moon. In fact, someone who has never seen the moon or its picture cannot *"imagine"* the real moon unless he actually sees it. In any other case, his mental representation of the moon will necessarily be inaccurate, false.

Likewise, when we speak of "Truth" or "Illusion" there is no way you can truly understand their meaning unless you actually experience them. This is why the Buddha advised his followers not to try to rationally understand his teachings or to stick to his words but to try to see beyond instead:

The Buddha said:

"My teaching is like a finger pointing to the moon. Do not mistake the finger for the moon."

As this simile states, *"reality"* cannot be expressed with words. Anything you believe or say about it is only *"a finger pointing to the moon"*.

And since all words are merely *"fingers pointing to the moon"*, we must be careful about what we think, say and believe. Don´t fall into the senseless trap of believing that your personal interpretation of reality is the absolute truth.

Don't be a fool for the finger is not the point…: the point is the moon!

RELATIVITY OF WORDS AND THOUGHTS

In certain parts of Thailand and Africa, the natives hold peculiar beliefs and values regarding beauty. Their particular ideal of female beauty consists in elongated necks, produced by primitive neck-stretching techniques. To these girls there is only one Truth: *"The longer the better!"*

Stretching the girl's necks is a long and harsh process…

As early as the age of two, the small girls start wearing metal rings that are gradually increased in length and that actually stretch their necks a few inches in a matter of one or two decades. And the lifelong process never stops.

All these girls believe that the longer their necks are, the prettier they will look. They also believe that having a short neck is synonymous of *"ugliness"*. So they all have one big desire:

"Having the longest or one of the longest necks!"

This real-life example depicts what I call *"the relativity of beauty"*. Truth is, like the Greek philosopher Plato allegedly said:

"Beauty lies in the eyes of the beholder".

The ideal of beauty no only changes from place to place, but also from time to time. What we consider *"beautiful"* today doesn't necessarily mean it was considered *"beautiful"* in the past and vice versa.

In the early 1900's, for example, the female beauty ideal was mid-sized and a bit *"robust"* or *"chubby"* The most popular hairstyle at the time was a bob. And women *"bound their breasts"* to give themselves a more boyish figure. Back then, athletic, thin and strong females were simply not seen as *"beautiful"* or *"attractive"*, like today.

Take Mary Pickford, for example, the Canadian-American silent film actress and co-founder of the film studio United Artists. She was a very short and somewhat round-faced woman. Nevertheless, people at the time saw her as *"the most beautiful woman on earth"* and compared the shape of her face with *"the roundness of childhood"*.

Pickford's famous curls, according to the press at the time, made her look *"like a living doll"*. Everyone said *"the camera loved her"* and no actress before her had ever been loved more by her audience. In fact, she was considered so *"beautiful"* and *"charming"*, that she became the first movie actress known as *"America's sweetheart"* (an honor many decades later shared with Sandra Bullock, a real *"no-beauty"* according to 1900 standards).

Regarding the "relativity of beauty", the founder of Taoism, the philosopher and poet of ancient China Lao-Tzu (6th century BC) explained that as soon as you define *"beauty"* then *"ugliness"* is automatically defined. This occurs because our mind is ruled by *"duality"*, that is, in a world of *"opposite sides"*, in which everything is valued in terms of *"good"* and *"bad"*.

Let´s take a glance at what Lao-Tzu wrote over two thousand years ago in his celebrated masterpiece the *Tao Te King*:

> *"When people see some things as beautiful, other things become ugly. When people see some things as good, other things become bad... Under heaven all can see beauty as beauty only because there is ugliness. All can know good as good only because there is evil."*

To this, the celebrated Taoist master Chuang Tzu (4th century BC) added the following:

> *"Everyone has his own conception of beauty and therefore establishes ugliness. Everyone has his own conception of Goodness and therefore establishes evil".*

In any case, our personal appreciation of beauty and goodness will always depend on our personal beliefs, values and desires.

And, as we will see in this chapter, these are initially set in our early childhood and unconsciously and define our present personality and behavior.

ADOPTING BELIEFS, VALUES AND DESIRES

Let´s see how the interdependence between our beliefs, values and desires sets its roots in the mind of every child through a three-stage process:

1: Establishment of set of beliefs: As a child you receive a "set of beliefs" from your parents, relatives, teachers, friends and social environment, among others. These beliefs depend on your "mental chatter" to grow and become stronger. The more you think about them positively the stronger they will get.

For example:

"Long necks make women beautiful."

2: Establishment of scale of values: Based on those beliefs, as a child you unconsciously establish a "basic list or scale" of things that you believe are "good" and of thing that you believe are "bad". As a child, you will naturally "value" the "good things" more than the bad things. And the more you think about the things you most value, the stronger your scale of value swill be.

For example:

"Women with long necks are better and more valuable whereas those with short necks are worse and less valuable."

3: Establishment of personal desires: Finally, the more you "value" something, the more you will cherish or desire it. And the less you "value" it, the less you will want it. Also, "better" and "more valuable" things will always make you feel "good" and not having them will always you feel "bad".

It's plain to see that your personal desires depend on your personal set of values, and that these, in turn, depend on your personal set of beliefs.

For example:

If you accept that women with long necks are "better" than those with short ones, then you will surely experience one of these two desires:

1: *If I am a female, I will naturally desire a long neck.*

2: *If I am a male, I will naturally desire a woman with a long neck.*

And thus the personal desire for long necks is born!

THE NATURE OF ABSTRACT CONCEPTS

One of the most unwanted consequences of the prehistoric birth of human language together with what Eckhart calls our *"incessant stream of thinking*" is that our remote ancestors began thinking about everything and at all times, creating new words to describe all sorts of *"abstract concepts"* and *"speculations"*.

These include imaginary and abstract concepts such as justice, happiness, freedom, worthiness, beauty, glory, courage, goodness, realization, duty, merit, power, manners, legal, success and honor, among others.

Of course, these concepts differ from person to person, from place to place, and from time to time. And despite the fact that they are abstract and therefore non-existent, they affect our lives under the form of different beliefs, values and desires.

One of the abstract terms that has caused more problems is the concept of time, a direct consequence of the *"invention"* of the abstract words: *"past"*, *"present"* and *"future"*.

Among the most important abstract beliefs adopted by humans stand good and evil, better and worse, success and failure and happiness and unhappiness, to name a few.

THE ILLUSORY NATURE OF OUR BELIEFS

As we have seen, ever since you were a child, you have been collecting uncountable number of *"accepted beliefs"*.

These include countless cultural, religious, political and social beliefs that you initially *"learned"* from your parents, grandparents, and teachers, as well as from countless sources during your growing years and adulthood.

As you grow older, some beliefs may pass from being perceived as "*good*" and "*desired*" to "*bad*" and "*unwanted*". Others simply may turn out being wrong, like for example the ancient belief that the world was flat.

Since it looked flat, people thought it was flat. And for thousands of years that was the "*generally accepted truth*". But only until science proved them wrong.

Human history is full of examples of other "*accepted truths*" that were once widely accepted and that as time passed turned out to be "*false beliefs*" and even "*incoherent*" and "*absurd*".

Here are some examples of "*false beliefs*" that were once considered absolute truths. And the astounding list continues to grow:

> **The notion that our planet occupies the very center of the universe and that the sun, moon, stars and planets all revolve around us. (Geocentric astronomic theory).*

> **The theory that states that all human thinking takes place in the stomach (Aristotelian anatomy).*

*The notion that the world is flat and that if you sail far enough from the coast you will inevitably fall off its edge and perish (Medieval astronomy and navigation)

*The scientific theory that establishes that space and time truly exist and that they are absolute (Pre-Einstein mechanic physics).

*The belief in supernatural beings, dragons, ogres, gnomes, leprechauns, trolls, fairies, unicorns, centaurs, genies, werewolves, vampires, zombies, witches, trolls, and other imaginary creatures (Olden folk tales).

*The conviction that we control our minds instead of our unconscious (Pre-Freudian psychology)

*The practice of massively sacrificing humans as the most effective way to please the gods and obtain their favors, especially young virgins (Aztec religion).

*The notion that if God had wanted man to fly he would have given him wings (Popular saying before the invention of the airplane)

The legal permission to capture, buy and sell Afro-Americans and enslave them (USA before the Abolition of slavery)

The social norm that established that men in full dress occasions cannot be seen without wearing a wig diligently powdered to give it a distinctive white or off-white color (18th Century English etiquette)

The claim that Germany's Aryan race is "the world's superior race" and therefore must rule over the other races (Nazi philosophy).

And the list goes on and on...

These beliefs were doomed to perish. Surprisingly, they were considered undisputed truths by millions of people before being trashed.

So, what makes you sure that your beliefs are really true? How many of them are wrong without you or anyone else knowing it? Is there any guarantee that any of them are true?

The following principle answers the question:

If a belief is based on abstract concepts, then it won't have real essence and, wrong or right, it will only be an illusion.

THE ILLUSORY SCALE OF VALUES

As I explained earlier, based on our particular beliefs every one of us creates a personal scale of values by which "we measure all things".

They values are basically objective. That is, they depend on *"the eye of the beholder"* and are therefore unreal.

One way of evidencing that our values are not absolute and therefore unreal, is that your values are not the same as anyone else´s.

We all have different values because we all have different beliefs.

For example, the values of a samurai warrior practicing his art are not the same as the values of a Wall Street broker driving to work.

The values of the Dalai Lama giving a lecture are different from those of a Mafia hit-man holding his rifle.

And the values of an Australian aborigine throwing his boomerang to catch his prey has almost nothing to do with the values of an astronaut stationed for in the international space station for three or four months.

In any case, our values determine our behavior. And as experience shows, what's good for one person is often bad for another.

In Cambodia, for example, it is considered "an honor" to eat one of their most popular national dishes. Would you like to try it?

With so little information, I bet you still don't know what to "believe" about the Cambodian dish, and much less determine its value.

Let me give you another clue:

The Cambodian dish is often described as "crispy on the outside and with tender white meat inside, with a vague taste of chicken or cod". Now, would you like to try it?

I think the information is still not enough. And I bet you probably still don't know if you'd like to try it or not. Why? Because you still don't really know what the dish is and therefore still don't know what to believe. However, if you like crispy food and white meat, then perhaps you would like to try it. Or perhaps not.

I know I wouldn't.

Why?

Because the name of the popular Cambodian dish I'm talking about is: *Tarantula spiders in dipping sauce!*

Now that you know what's the dish, you may feel repulse, be indifferent, or your mouth will water.

Your desires will always depend on your personal set of beliefs and your particular scale of values. If you were Cambodian, as well as all your family, I bet you would have already tried it. And more than once!

Applying Albert Einstein's Theory of Relativity we can formulate the following principle:

> *All our beliefs, values and desires are relative and therefore unreal because they vary from person to person and they depend on relative and erroneous perceptions and points of views.*

ILLUSORY CRAVINGS AND DESIRES

Just as our beliefs give birth to our scale of values, with which we *"measure all things"*, our scale of values gives birth to our cravings and desires.

According to the teachings of the Buddha, *"pain or suffering arises through desire or craving"*. And desires and cravings, according to what we have seen, arise from the *"chatter in our minds"*.

Hinduism teaches us that unfulfilled desires cause suffering and that the more desires we have and wish to fulfill, the more we suffer when they remain unfulfilled. Therefore, freedom from desires always leads to freedom from suffering. This is why Buddha said that *"to be free of pain we need to cut the bonds of desire"*.

However, freeing ourselves from desire doesn´t mean not having any more desires. Of course we can have desires, like reading this book, for instance, or wanting to go out for dinner tonight. But we should not allow ourselves to be bound to our desires. See the difference?

The secret to overcoming desire is not to lose all our desires, but to transform all our binding desires into non-binding ones. And you can only achieve this by draining the power from your ego and taking the reins of your life in your own hands. Be Present". Be there as the observer of the mind. Instead of quoting the Buddha, be the Buddha, be *"the awakened one,"* which is what the word Buddha truly means."

The Secret of Now Series

DO NOT BELIEVE
Buddha

"Do not believe in anything
simply because you have heard it.
Do not believe in anything
simply because it is spoken
and rumoured by many.

Do not believe in anything
simply because it is found
written in your religious books.

Do not believe in anything
merely on the authority of
your teachers and elders.

Do not believe in traditions
because they have been
handed down for many generations.

But after observation and analysis,
when you find that anything
agrees with reason and is
conducive to the good and
benefit of one and all,
then accept it and live up to it."

(The Anguttara Nikaya)

* * *

FIFTH EXERCISE

EXPERIENCING YOUR INNER BODY

"Direct your attention into the body. Feel it from within. Is it alive? Is there life in your hands, arms, legs, and feet - in your abdomen, your chest? Can you feel the subtle energy field that pervades the entire body and gives vibrant life to every organ and every cell? Can you feel it simultaneously in all parts of the body as a single field of energy? Keep focusing on the feeling of your inner body for a few moments. Do not start to think about it. Feel it. The more attention you give it, the clearer and stronger this feeling will become."

Eckhart Tolle

ECKHART TOLLE RECOMMENDS "experiencing presence" as one way of slowing down your thoughts and begin to stop the never-ending *"mental chatter"*. And that's the basis of this exercise.

According to Eckhart, to experience presence you must keep in mind the following two basic principles:

> *The body is "the vehicle for experiencing presence".*
>
> *"You cannot experience presence in your mind".*

The following exercise is one way of experiencing presence. Just follow these steps:

1: Close your eyes and concentrate on "feeling" your hands. Try to feel a "tingling" or "warmth" within them. You can do it if you concentrate enough. You will soon feel it. Eckhart calls this tingling or warmth "your inner sense of aliveness".

It is your inner presence and being-ness, the *'you'* that you really are, that is, you natural, inner consciousness or Self. Concentrate. Feel it. Experience it.

2: Once you have experienced the "tingling" or "warmth" in your hands, then proceed to observe your thoughts, as you did in the previous exercises. Close your eyes. No matter what you're thinking, realize that you are having a thought and identify it. Once you recognize it, say "yes" out loud and, without engaging in your first thought, leave it for later and let it go as before.

3: As soon as you release you last thought, take your attention away from thinking and concentrate in your hands. Feel the warmth or the inner tingling of its energy (its "aliveness"). Concentrate on this feeling and also experience the "gap".

This will certainly help you help you slow down your thoughts. Although Eckhart recommends focusing on the hands, it really doesn't matter what part of your body you focus on. What's important is that you take your focus **away** from your thoughts and focus on something physical.

By taking your focus and attention away from your thoughts and placing it on something physical (and therefore more "real") you will be able to slow down your mind and silence your thoughts, allowing you to experience the "gaps".

4: Try to keep mental silence. Be the Observer, that is, your Self. Sooner or later "the voice inside your head" will throw in a new thought. Recognize it as something different that your Self. Recognize it as your "ego". And as soon as you have an idea, recognize it, say "yes" and let it go, before concentrating once more in the tingling or warmth of your hands.

5: Do this with different parts of your body until you manage to experience your complete inner body as a whole. Try to feel the subtle energy field that pervades your entire body and gives vibrant life to every organ and every cell and also try to feel it simultaneously in all parts of the body as a single field of energy. As you concentrate on what you feel, keep your mind blank and continue observing your thoughts. Every time a new thought arrives, observe it, recognize it and let it go - leave it for later. Then immediately concentrate in the tingling of your inner body and experience the "gap".

6: Repeat this process several times (for one or two minutes) and try to do this exercise several times a day. It will allow you to get in touch with what Eckhart calls "your inner sense of aliveness". This, as he says, is the subtle sense of aliveness and concentrating on it is a great way of bringing your awareness to the present moment!

LESSON 6

THE ILLUSION OF TIME

"The secret of health for both mind and body is not to mourn for the past, nor to worry about the future, but to live the present moment wisely and earnestly."

Gautama Buddha

ACCORDING TO ALBERT EINSTEIN, *"time is an illusion"*. In fact, his famous Theory of Relativity proved that "time is always relative" and that "absolute time" does not exist. In other words, that what we call time is really "our own relative perception" and is therefore only "an illusion".

It took Einstein years of hard work to reach this conclusion. Before his work, scientists believed time was absolute and that it elapsed with the same speed here, there and everywhere in the universe. But he proved them wrong!

Sixteen years after Einstein's death, a group of scientists conducted a series of experiments to determine if Einstein was right or not regarding the relativity of time and its physical inexistence. It must be said that back then many distinguished scientists still believed time existed and that what he claimed was impossible!

One of the most polemical principles they publicly rejected was that, according to Einstein, *the faster you go, the slower time passes*.

This was utter madness, they cried out: "Time is a universal phenomenon, Einstein is wrong!" their clearly stated. "Time passes at the same speed everywhere! Always at the same speed, here and in the furthest corner of creation! If not, this universe would not exist!"

THE TIME DILATION EXPERIMENTS

During October, 1971, a group of scientists led by Joseph C.

Hafele, a physicist, and Richard E. Keating set out to prove that Einstein was right. Their work is known as the "time dilation experiments".

First, Hafele and Keating got hold of three macroscopic clocks, that is, cesium atomic beam clocks capable of measuring down to one nanosecond, which is one billionth of a second.

Second, they needed to find two turbo jets capable of flying at high speed. They wanted to leave one of the macroscopic clocks on land and fly the other two at high speed to see if there was the most minimal change.

If Einstein was right, there would be a slight difference between the clock left on land and the other two, which would allegedly "tick" slower.

The best solution they could find was flying them on commercial jet flights around the world twice, once eastward and once westward. And that's what they did.

According to the U.S. Naval Observatory, the flying clocks lost 59+/-10 nanoseconds during the eastward trip and gained 273+/-7 nanosecond during the westward trip. This proved that, effectively, time is not an absolute value but a relative one and therefore has no real essence.

Like Einstein said, *"time is an illusion"*!

THE THREE TENSES OF TIME

Back in the Stone Age, the abstract concept of time shook mankind. A mere invention it was. But it still has not ceased to shake us all!

Never before had such a tremendous power been released by a single word.

Based on primitive logic, the concept of time was developed based on three other abstract concepts that shook the world:

1: Now

2: Before

3: After

Presently known as:

1: Present.

2: Past

3: Future

Just like the apparent movement of the sun across the sky and the apparent flatness of the earth, the apparent march of time also fooled our ancestors when they began to create abstract concepts and beliefs based on their own reasoning.

If we examine each one of time's three tenses we will find the following:

1: The future has not taken place. So it still doesn't exist.

2: The past already took place. So it has ceased to exist.

3: And the present passes by so fast that by the time you say "this is the present" it's not the same present anymore!

These three tenses are the basis of what is known as "psychological time" which only exists in our minds.

THE NOW IS EVER PRESENT

Apart from psychological time, there exists the ever-present Now, as Krishnamurti explains in his *Colllected Works (Vol. IV,12)*:

> *"The present is the eternal. Through time, the timeless is not experienced. 'The now' is ever existent; even if you escape into future,'the now' is ever present. The present is the doorway to the past. If you do not understand the present now, will you understand it in the future? What you are now you will be, if the present is not understood.*

Understanding comes only through the present: postponement does not yield comprehension.

"Time is transcended only in the stillness of the present. This tranquility is not to be gained through time, through 'becoming' tranquil; there must be stillness, not the becoming still. We look to time as a means to become. This becoming is endless: it is not the eternal, the timeless. The becoming is endless conflict, leading to illusion. In the stillness of the present is the eternal.

"The now is ever existent; even if you escape into future, the now is ever present through becoming tranquil…"

BREAK FREE FROM PSYCHOLOGICAL TIME

When we speak of being in the present moment we are not talking about the psychological present. Why? Because there is a clear distinction between psychological time and what we call "chronological time".

Psychological time, as Eckhart Tolle explains, *"is identification with the past and continuous compulsive projection into the future… The enlightened persons main focus of attention is always the Now, but they are still peripherally aware of time. In other words, they continue to use clock time but are free of psychological time."*

According to him, psychological time has generated a mental disease in humans, who believe they can build a better future and that the end justifies the means. This is why most humans are always trying to get somewhere other than where they are and basing their lives in finding a means to this end.

They are not satisfied with their present lives. They imagine a better future, a better "them", and experience life as if their happiness is always waiting just around the corner. And nevertheless, no matter how much they try, they are never able to truly find nor grasp it.

JESUS AND LIVING IN THE NOW

Jesus highlighted the importance of not being trapped in psychological time in his celebrated Sermon of the Mount, in which he said, as Mathew 6 states:

> *"You are the salt of the earth; but if the salt loses its flavor, how shall it be seasoned? It is then good for nothing but to be thrown out and trampled underfoot by men.*
>
> *"You are the light of the world. A city that is set on a hill cannot be hidden. Nor do they*

light a lamp and put it under a basket, but on a lampstand, and it gives light to all who are in the house.

"Let your light so shine before men, that they may see your good works and glorify your Father in heaven.

Let go of your past

"You have heard that it was said to those of old, 'You shall not murder, and whoever murders will be in danger of the judgment.' But I say, even if you are angry with someone, you are subject to judgment! And whoever says to his brother, 'Idiot!' shall be in danger of the court. But whoever curses someone shall be in danger of the fires of hell.

"Therefore if you bring your gift to the altar, and there remember that your brother has something against you, leave your gift there before the altar, and go your way.

"First be reconciled to your brother, and then come and offer your gift. Agree with your adversary quickly, while you are on the way with him, lest your adversary deliver you

to the judge, the judge hand you over to the officer, and you be thrown into prison.

"Assuredly, I say to you, you will by no means get out of there till you have paid the last penny.

Don't worry about the future

"Therefore I say to you, do not worry about your life, what you will eat or what you will drink; nor about your body, what you will put on.

"Is not life more than food and the body more than clothing?

"Look at the birds of the air, for they neither sow nor reap nor gather into barns; yet your heavenly Father feeds them.

"Are you not of more value than they?

"Which of you by worrying can add one cubit to his stature?

"So why do you worry about clothing?

"Consider the lilies of the field, how they grow: they neither toil nor spin; and yet I say to you that even Solomon in all his glory was not arrayed like one of these.

"Now if God so clothes the grass of the field, which today is, and tomorrow is thrown into the oven, will He not much more clothe you, O you of little faith?

"Therefore do not worry, saying: 'What shall we eat?' or 'What shall we drink?' or 'What shall we wear?' For after all these things the Gentiles seek. For your heavenly Father knows that you need all these things. But seek first the kingdom of God and His righteousness, and all these things shall be added to you.

"Therefore do not worry about tomorrow, for tomorrow will worry about its own things. Enough for each day is its own trouble."

AN OPTICAL DELUSION OF CONSCIOUSNESS
Albert Einstein

A human being is part of the whole so-called universe... We experience ourselves, our thoughts and feelings as something separate from the rest (from the universe). A kind of optical delusion of consciousness!

This delusion is a kind of prison for us, restricting us to our personal desires and to affection for a few persons nearest to us.

Our task must be to free ourselves from the prison by widening our circle of compassion to embrace all living creatures and the whole of nature in its beauty (the whole universe).

The true value of a human being is determined by the measure and the sense in which they have obtained liberation from the self. We shall require a substantially new manner of thinking if humanity is to survive.

a twist when his "listening game" switched from the outer sounds of nature to the inner sound of his breath.

Concentrating on his breath, his "inner chatter" diminished and ceased.

The young boy went into trance!

And thus, he spontaneously "discovered" the science of breath meditation.

According to the ancient scriptures, "all the conditions conducive to quiet meditation being there, the pensive child, young in years but old in wisdom, sat cross-legged and seized the opportunity to commence that all-important practice of intense concentration on the breath -on exhalations and inhalations- which gained for him then and there that one-pointedness of mind known as Samadhi (a glimpse of oneness or mindfulness) and he thus developed the first jhäna (ecstasy)."

After abandoning their duty to enjoy themselves at the festival for who knows how long, the maids returned and found the young prince sitting cross-legged, plunged in deep meditation.

It is said that when the boy's parents returned, they found him meditating in deep trance and that he never forgot what he did that day.

Many years later, when seeking realization, he left his home and spent six years with a group of ascetic monks or "sadhus", who practiced the Hindu way of renunciation or *"sanyasa"*. Hoping to find enlightenment, he lived like a mendicant (beggar) and encouraged abstinence and self-mortification. However, as time passed, he realized the futility of his efforts.

Disillusioned and invaded with deep sorrow, one morning he left the ascetics and continued his search for spiritual realization on his own. And it is said that shortly after he was resting under a Bodhi tree when he remembered his experience at the Plowing Festival, when he was only a child. And thus he discovered what is presently known as the cornerstone of Buddhist meditation, which led him to Nirvana or enlightenment.

BREATHING MEDITATION EXERCISE

I learned this basic meditation technique when I was seventeen. It´s very simple. To practice it, just follow these steps:

1: Sit or lie down in a comfortable and relaxing position. The position you now have while reading this book will do. You can also adopt another one or maybe a meditation or yoga pose.

2: Close your eyes and listen to the sound of your breath. That will be your "mantra" or "sacred word". Listen to your breath. Don´t control it, just listen and be the Observer.

3: If a thought arises, observe it, understand it and let it go. Try to feel the "gaps" between each thought.

4: To slow down your thoughts, listen to the sound of your breath and also "feel" the movement of your lungs, the movement of your chest and abdomen slowly expanding and contracting as the air moves in and out… Don´t try to control your breath. Let it go. Be the Observer. Concentrate. Feel it. Experience it. "One conscious breath is enough to make some space where before there was the uninterrupted succession of one thought after another."

5: Repeat the process as each new thought arises. Don´t reject them. Observe them, let them go and concentrate on your breath. Realize that breathing isn't something you do but something you witness or observe. Breathing is autonomous and effortless. Your unconscious inner intelligence is in charge of it. Just be the Observer. Just be the Witness. If you slow down your "inner chat" and experience the gaps between thoughts, you won't lose yourself in your thoughts and will experience the Now.

6: Repeat this exercise as often as you can. Combine them with the others. Work on one a few days and on another, until you find the one that best suits you according to your capacity and level of practice.

The Secret of Now Series

LEVEL THREE:
THE MASTER

Mastering the Art of Being Present

With due knowledge and sufficient practice always comes Mastery. Once the practitioner masters the ancient art of Being Present in the Now, the inner Self or Being gradually surges from within and can be personally felt –though never understood intellectually. When practicing the Art of Being Present, advanced practitioners may experience occasional "altered states of consciousness" as well as "non-dual states of consciousness". Known in Hinduism as "Savikalpa Samadhi", these altered states of consciousness are often described as states of "Beingness", that is, of "being aware of one's existence without thinking", characterized by bliss (ananda) and joy (sukha). This process implies regaining awareness of our inner Being and being continuously Present in the Now, enjoying an internalized state of awareness and inner peace often described as "awakened consciousness" or "enlightenment".

LESSON 7

A TRIP BACK HOME

"Many who seek quietness of mind withdraw from active life to a village, to a monastery, to the mountains, or they withdraw into ideas, enclose themselves in a belief or avoid people who give them trouble. Such isolation is not stillness of mind. The enclosure of the mind in an idea or the avoidance of people who make life complicated does not bring about stillness of mind. Stillness of mind comes only when here is no process of isolation through accumulation but complete understanding of the whole process of relationship...

"In that stillness, there is no formulation, there is no idea, there is no memory; that stillness is a state of creation that can be experienced only when there is complete understanding of the whole process of the `me'. Otherwise, stillness has no meaning. Only in that stillness, which is not a result, is the eternal discovered, which is beyond time."

Krishnamurti

IF YOU MANAGED TO REACH THIS LESSON, I assume that you have practiced all the previous exercises presented in this workbook. These, together with the theory contained in each lesson, are basically all you will need to get started.

Remember that according to Eckhart, the number and duration of the gaps between thoughts will increase with practice and will get more intense.

One more thing: If you are looking for spiritual progress, don't expect to find "rational" or "logical" answers to all your questions. Spiritual progress doesn't depend on intellectual knowledge.

Like the Buddha once said:

> *"Suppose a man is struck by a poisoned arrow and the doctor wishes to take out the arrow immediately. Suppose the man does not want the arrow removed until he knows who shot it, his age, his parents, and why he shot it. What would happen? If he were to wait until all these questions have been answered, the man might die first."*

MEISTER ECKHART AND LIVING IN THE NOW

Remember to live in the Now keeping in mind what seven centuries ago the Dominican monk known as Meister Eckhart expressed:

"Nothing in all creation is so like God as stillness."

"Time is what keeps the light from reaching us. There is no greater obstacle to God than time: and not only time but temporalities, not only temporal things but temporal affections, not only temporal affections but the very taint and smell of time…

"Spirituality is not to be learned by flight from the world, or by running away from things, or by turning solitary and going apart from the world. Rather, we must learn an inner solitude wherever or with whomsoever we may be. We must learn to penetrate things and find God there (and Now)…"

FINAL FREEDOM FROM MENTAL SLAVERY

If you identify yourself with your *"chattering mind"*, you will become a *"slave"* of your own mind. Like Ramana Maharshi said: *"The mind is Maya."* So use Maya to free yourself from illusion. *The* only way to realize that you are truly a slave of your mind and that you must free yourself from its influence is by following the ancient maxim inscribed in the Temple of Apollo at Delphi: *"Know thyself".*

That's basically it: *You need Self-knowledge. You need to observe your mind. You need to experience inner stillness. You need to "live in the Now".* If not, then you will forever sink in the quicksand of delusion, experiencing unhappiness, sadness, fear, rage and powerlessness, doomed to *"see only what the veil of Maya wants you to see."*

Removing the veil of Maya and seeing what lies behind it takes knowledge, practice, strength and courage. Hindu sages and gurus often compare it with taking "a trip back home". And so, my fellow reader, as our planet spins and travels, as the stars continue shining, profoundly sink in the "present moment" and you'll be on your way back home...

NAMASTE!

The Secret of Now Series

THE AWAKENED ONE

Do not seek outside your head.
Observe your mind.
Don't think about doing "this" or "that".
Simply become present.
Do it now.
Be the "Observer of the mind".
Be the Buddha.
Be "The Awakened One"

* * *

SEVENTH EXERCISE

THE AWAKENING TECHNIQUE

"Transformation is not in the future, can never be in the future. It can only be now, from moment to moment. So what do we mean by transformation? Surely it is very simple: seeing the false as the false and the true as the true. Seeing the truth in the false and seeing the false in that which has been accepted as the truth. Seeing the false as the false and the true as the true is transformation, because when you see something very clearly as the truth, that truth liberates. When you see that something is false, that false thing drops away.

"When you see that ceremonies are mere vain repetitions, when you see the truth of it and do not justify it, there is transformation, is there not?, because another bondage is gone. When you see that class distinction is false, that it creates conflict, creates misery, division between people - when you see the truth of it, that very truth liberates. The very perception of that truth is transformation, is it not?

"As we are surrounded by so much that is false, perceiving the falseness from moment to moment is transformation. Truth is not cumulative. It is from moment to moment. That which is cumulative, accumulated, is memory, and through memory you can never find truth, for memory is of time - time being the past, the present and the future. Time, which is continuity, can never find that which is eternal; eternity is not continuity. That which endures is not eternal. Eternity is in the moment. Eternity is in the now. The now is not the reflection of the past nor the continuance of the past through the present to the future."

Krishnamurti

THE AWAKENING TECHNIQUE IS a powerful *mini-meditation* that actually allows us to temporarily interrupt our "mental chatter" at will, that is, anytime and anywhere we want or need to!

Once you learn this technique it will be relatively easy for you to apply it whenever you wish! I use it almost every day. More than a technique for reaching enlightenment, it is a powerful way to stop our "mental chatter" (at least temporarily) allowing us to briefly experience inner stillness and peace.

I recommend it in case of emergencies, when we are facing a stressful situation and we urgently need to stop our own "mental chatter" and take a break from excessive thinking! We can stop our monologue, at least for a few minutes, while we relax and "recharge batteries". And we can also use this technique to "boost" your concentration when practicing "mantra meditation" or "breath meditation".

A BREAKTHROUGH TECHNIQUE

The Awakening Technique can actually help you by slowing down and even disappearing your "inner chat" when you most need to. It will also allow you to "recharge" yourself by giving yourself a break and not thinking for a few minutes.

I have found that it is the ideal practical and immediate solution when you find yourself:

*Excessively "tied up" in your own thoughts and can't stop thinking.

*Excessively disappointed with something, someone or yourself.

*Excessively worried about someone, something or yourself.

*Excessively angry at someone, something or yourself.

*Excessively sad about someone, something or yourself.

*Excessively excited about something, someone, or yourself.

*Excessively confused about someone, something, or yourself.

*Excessively afraid of someone or something.

*Excessively insomniac.

*Excessively discouraged.

*Excessively depressed.

*Excessively nervous.

In sum, The Awakening Technique can actually help you *ANY TIME YOU NEED TO STOP YOUR INNER CHAT!*

THE TECHNIQUE'S BASIC STEPS.

1: Sit or lie down in a comfortable and relaxing position. The position you now have while reading this book will do. You can also adopt another one or maybe a meditation or yoga pose.

2: Close your eyes. Listen to your breath or mentally repeat the universal mantra Om, whichever suits you best. Whatever you choose, that "sound" or "mantra" will be your "Stimulus Number One". Remember that.

3: Listen to your mantra (breath or Om) and as soon as a new thought arrives you know what to do: observe it, understand it, let it go and get back to repeating the mantra. But this time we will add a second stimulus.

4: As you continue "listening" to your mantra (breath or Om) gently touch the tips of your thumbs with the tips of you index fingers and gently rub them, with minimal movements, minimal frictions, minimal rubs. This sensation or feeling will be your "Stimulus Number Two". Remember that.

5: Concentrate on the sound of your mantra (breath or Om) and at the same time feel the tip of your fingers rubbing. This double-feeling will help you slow down your thoughts. Nevertheless, a new thought is bound to appear. When it does, recognize it, let it go and get back to feeling the mantra (breath or Om) and the sensation of your fingers rubbing. And now you are ready to add your third and last stimulus.

6: You will really need to concentrate to do this step. But once you master it you will find that it is really quite simple. And, as you will see, it has countless applications.

Concentrate. Listen to your mantra (breath or Om) and at the same time concentrate on the feeling of your fingers rubbing.

Try to feel both stimuli at the same time, can you?

If not, please return to the last step and repeat it until you succeed. It's really not that hard. A bit of practice will do.

If you do manage to perceive the sound of the mantra and the touch of your fingers at the same time, you're ready to add the third and last stimulus that will definitely stop your "inner chat":

7: Don't stop concentrating on the first two stimuli (mantra and fingers) and simply add the third stimulus:

Listen to all the sounds that surround you.

It can be the birds chirping or whatever's on the radio or TV. Or maybe some dogs barking or vehicles passing by. Whatever you hear will do. It can be children playing, cars honking, cows mooing, or your favorite music playing. It can be whatever you hear at that moment, as long that it is a real external sound. That will do.

7. Concentrate on the three stimuli at the same time. It takes so much concentration that you will virtually have no space for thinking. If you have a thought it's only because you stopped concentrating on one of the three stimulus, maybe two or even all. If you do, I figure by now you know what to do: Observe your thought, understand what it's about, leave it for later, let it go and continue concentrating on your three stimuli at the same time:

*Your sacred mantra (Internal Sound).

*Your sense of touch (Fingers Rubbing)

*Your sense of hearing (External Sound).

8: Practice this exercise at least twice a day. If you manage to experience the three stimuli at the same time, you will certainly experience brief gaps of non-thinking almost immediately (guaranteed). This is simple because our conscious minds find it hard to consciously pay complete attention to three things at the same time. So taking advantage of this "disadvantage", we are able to defeat our wandering and ever-chattering mind, forcing it to shut up at least for short periods of time or "gaps" that become longer with practice, as Eckhart Tolle and Deepak Chopra claim. And these "gaps", as they explain, are the gateway for living in the Now and for definitely entering the Path of Self-Realization and Enlightenment.

OTHER COMBINATIONS:

Remember, this technique works by combining three different stimuli, like for example listening to the sounds around you, feeling something with your fingers and chewing gum. As long as there are at least three, it will work.

Here are other possible stimuli you can use (combine 3):

*Feel the tingling of your hands.

*Feel the tingling of your whole body.

*Gently rub, caress or scratch any part of your body.

*Press or rub your tongue against your lower teeth.

*Hold your hands together and feel their contact.

*Hold your hands in praying position and fell their contact.

*Smell a penetrating fragrance like aromatic incense.

*Play some spiritual or meditation music.

*Pinch yourself anywhere you like.

*Feel the water as you take a shower or bath.

*Eat and slowly taste delicious food.

*Enjoy sexual intercourse without saying a word.

EVERYDAY USE OF THE TECHNIQUE:

I use The Awakening Technique almost every day. Especially when I'm walking around somewhere or waiting in line for a while.

No matter where you are or what you are doing you can use The Awakening Technique to "anchor" yourself in the present moment and stop your "inner conversation with yourself". Here's what you need to do:

1: If you are walking, for example, or driving or standing in line, gently rub the tip of your thumb and index finger and concentrate on feeling this sensation (We will call it Stimulus One). If you're driving, you can gently rub the steering wheel with minimal movements if you like, making it imperceptible to anyone who sees you doing it.

2: As you rub your fingertips, press or rub the tip off your tongue against your lower teeth. Feel this and also feel the tips of your fingers rubbing. Rubbing your teeth with your tongue will also be imperceptible to anyone who sees you or who you're driving with. One you feel both stimuli at the same time you are ready for the final step.

3: As you continue feeling the touch of your finger or fingers, together with the sensation of your tongue rubbing against your teeth add the third and final stimulus:

Listen to all the sounds that surround you.

It can be the birds chirping or whatever's on the radio or TV. Or maybe some dogs barking or vehicles passing by. Whatever you hear will do. It can be children playing, cars honking, cows mooing, or your favorite music playing. It can be whatever you hear at that moment, as long that it is a real external sound. That will do.

As you listen to all the sounds that surround you, continue feeling the touch of your finger or fingers, together with the sensation of your tongue rubbing against your teeth.

4. Concentrate on the three stimuli at the same time. It will takes so much concentration that you won't have space for thinking. If you do have a thought it's only because you stopped perceiving one of the three stimulus, or maybe two or even all. And if this happens, you know what to do: Observe your thought, understand what it's about, leave it for later, let it go and continue concentrating on your three stimuli.

WHEN CAN YOU USE THIS TECHNIQUE?

The Awakening Technique basically "keeps you awake", that is, it instantaneously and effectively diminishes your normal train of thoughts and allows you to "be present". Where can you use it? Anywhere!

I normally use it when:

Walking

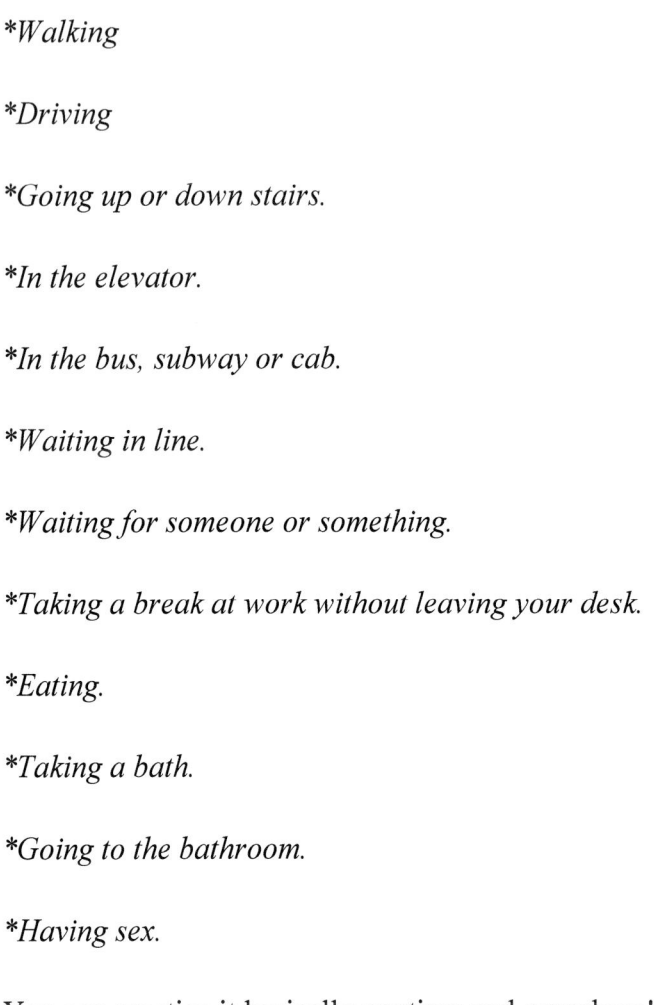

Driving

Going up or down stairs.

In the elevator.

In the bus, subway or cab.

Waiting in line.

Waiting for someone or something.

Taking a break at work without leaving your desk.

Eating.

Taking a bath.

Going to the bathroom.

Having sex.

You can practice it basically anytime and anywhere!

Do it now! Slow down your "inner chat", start to experience the "gaps" between thoughts described by Eckhart and Chopra, and immerse yourself in the Power of Now!

ABOUT THE AUTHOR

IN MY OWN WORDS

(A. J. PARR is an experienced journalist and author with a lifelong interest in meditation techniques and the Comparative Study of Religion)

When I was 17 years old (I am now 58) I received my first Hindu initiation at the Mission of the Divine Light, founded by Guru Maharaj Ji (presently known as Prem Rawat or Maharaji). His basic teachings or "Knowledge", based on ancient Hinduism and Buddhism, included four meditation techniques (Divine Light, Inner Music, Word and Nectar) to help us stop the mind and free ourselves from Illusion.

I was 30 when I received my second Hindu initiation and meditation technique, this time from a disciple of Maharishi Mahesh Yogi (1918-2008), creator of Transcendental Meditation or TM.

Maharishi´s "mantra meditation" technique was practiced, among others, by the Beatles, Mia Farrow, Shirley MacLaine, Donovan, and also Deepak Chopra, who worked side by side with Maharishi before starting his own career a spiritual guide. And, according to him, he still practices it and widely recommends it for attaining inner peace and spiritual progress.

I was 37when I received my third initiation and meditation technique. This time from a disciple of guru Sant Thakar Singh (1929–2005) of the Sant Mat tradition, which is also known as "The Path of Saints". The Indian poet and saint Kabir (1440–1518) belonged to the first generation of Sant Mat, which is derived from Hinduism and influenced by Sikhism.

I was also a Freemason for three years (1987-1990) and around ten years ago, while studying "A Course in Miracles", I became acquainted with the teachings of Eckhart Tolle, which I have practiced since then and more recently gave birth to *"The Secret of Now Series"*:

The Secret of Now Series

PUBLISHED BY:

GRAPEVINE BOOKS
Copyright © A.J. Parr 2016
All Rights Reserved
Contact the Author:
edicionesdelaparra@gmail.com

Printed in Great Britain
by Amazon